Poetry From Pain

A Black Man's Story

Maximus

Published By

P E A C H E S

P U B L I C A T I O N S

Published in London by Peaches Publications, 2021.
www.peachespublications.co.uk

The moral right of the author has been asserted.

All rights reserved. No part of this book may be reproduced, stored in a retrieval system, or transmitted in any form or by any means, electronic, mechanical, photocopying, recording, public performances or otherwise, without written permission of Maxwell Johnson, except for brief quotations embodied in critical articles or reviews. The book is for personal use only; commercial use is prohibited unless written permission and a license is obtained from the author Maxwell Johnson.

The right of Maxwell Johnson to be identified as the author of this work has been asserted in accordance with sections 77 and 78 of the copyright Designs and Patents Act 1988.

Text Copyright © 2021 Maxwell Johnson.

British Library Cataloguing in Publication Data: A catalogue record for this book is available from the British Library.

ISBN: 9798502634083.

Book cover design: Peaches Publications.
Front Cover Artwork: Marlon Francis.
Typesetter: Winsome Duncan.
Proof reader: Joanna Oliver.

Table of Contents

Dedication 10
In Memory 11
Acknowledgements 12
Introduction 13
Black Man's Struggle 15
    God's Son 16
    Black Man 18
    The Struggles of a Black Man living in England
    19
    Rejected 21
    Bully Boss 22
    Great Heist 23
    Kindness for Weakness 25
Overcoming 27
    Still I Rise 28
    False Reality 29
    The Clever Monkey 31
    The Refugee 32
    Wheel of Life 33
Deep and Spiritual 35
    Trials 36

This World	37
I Didn't Listen	39
The Lost Soul	41
Inhuman	42
Star Seed	43
A Poet's Journey	**45**
My Pen	46
Poet	47
Keep Going	48
On Reflection	50
Alone	51
My Advice	52
Relationships and Love	**53**
Imperfectly Perfect	54
Who Wins?	55
Set the Rabbit Free	57
Travel	**59**
The Traveller	60
Black Man in Thailand	61
Scraping the Sky	63
Ethiopian Goddess	65
Freedom	**67**
Jamaican Sunrise	68

- A New Age 69
- Finally Free 70
- Family Ties 73
  - Mother's Day 74
  - Grandma 75
- Old Skool Rhymes 76
  - Blame Satan 77
  - No Love 79
  - R.I.P Souljah 81
  - Ancestors' Blood 83
  - Fed Up 84
  - The Eye of the Hurricane 86
- About the Author 87
- Epilogue 88
- Reflection Notes 89

Dedication

This book is dedicated to all of the ancestors, teachers and Ascended Masters who fought valiantly in order for us to sip from the cup of freedom. We need you.

In Memory

In loving memory of all my fallen Warriors. R.I.P.

Acknowledgements

I would like to thank my parents for life and your teachings along with my siblings, dear friends and family, past teachers, mentors, and everyone that has helped Maximus throughout this journey. Life is full of losses and lessons and these people gave me the power, strength and wisdom when I needed it most.

A very special thanks also extends to Owen Rennalls, Rosemary Harris, Kate Vaughan, Bev Campbell, Marlon Francis, Tyrese Johnson Fisher, Tara Johnson, Natika Hamilton, Denny Carty, J.Biz, C.Money along with my proof reader Joanna Oliver and publisher Winsome Duncan. Your past and ongoing support has been instrumental in the completion of this heartfelt project.

Lastly, I would like to thank the most high for all of the love and blessings that you have bestowed on me. I appreciate you.

Introduction

As a young black man growing up in South London, Maximus struggled to make a life for himself. Despite the daily struggles, his journey inspired him to be resilient. After numerous attempts to find a suitable profession, he has found himself exploring the world around him through the lens of the art of poetry and story-telling, an art he is now using to address issues affecting black people and general societal problems.

When you are feeling voiceless, hopeless, or like you do not have any rights, it can be difficult to believe that life is ever going to be any better. How can it be better if you are facing adversity, disrespect and worse, simply because of the way you look? What can you do if you struggle, not because of something you did but because of your ethnicity? Is there a way to find meaning in all of your suffering and perhaps even to learn how to stand strong and brave, in spite of the difficulties you are experiencing?

Divided into nine sections, this collection, 'Poetry from Pain- the Black Man's Story' deals with the trials and tribulations Maximus experiences as a black man in London. The book transcends wide-ranging themes including love and relationships, travel and loss, providing spiritual insights that may also help you to find your own strength to overcome whatever circumstances you are facing.

Black Man's Struggle

God's Son

I watched as my dreams disappeared in the mist,
I saw people living my life and I was pissed,
I couldn't react and I was far from a lift,
then God came along and revealed a little gift.
He said, "Son I have blessed you with the power of the Word,
You've got a handsome face plus the brain of a nerd
and during your time on earth, I would prefer if you used your talents wisely, so peace can occur",
I observed, listened intently to his verse
Thought about my daily struggles
and not getting my just desserts,
Thought if you really loved me,
How could you let me taste the dirt?
Too many times been undermined,
The world's unkind,
This doesn't work.

But then he spoke to me again
And said, "son I feel your pain,
You think I didn't see you struggle?
Gave you life, I gave you game.
You think I didn't see you hustle
And get knocked time and again?
You think I didn't see the hatred,
From old bosses to ex-friends?
But I did.

And you did.

Make me proudest in tough moments,
I only make you go through trials
So, you align with all the hopeless.
I only make them cross that line,
For you to fuel a rhyme so potent.
Teach 'em 'best things come from struggle,'
Through your story,
they will know this".

Black Man

His life is real complex,
See him, they start to judge,
Frustration turns to anger,
'Respect before the love'.

A playing field uneven,
A path where many fell,
Then crucified by media,
Who taught, he'd "give them hell".

A curse and many felt it,
From jobs to names on streets,
Where charges were invalid,
in deaths, involve police.

A stunning contribution,
Read books,
And maybe then,
You'll see him for his greatness,
One love to all black men.

The Struggles of a Black Man living in England

If you're a Black man living in England,
you can expect to face lots of opposition.
Your life is worthless, unless,
someone can make a pound from you.
You'll wait hours in queues before being tended to,
It's almost like you are   invisible,
like no one sees you until
the police are "cutting down on crimes."
Now all of a sudden, you're the grand prize,
the one everyone can't wait to get their hands on.
That's why you're nine times more likely to be stopped and searched
because they see your birth
and very existence as a threat,
to the notion 'supremacy'.
It's no wonder a Black man struggles to land a top-rated job.
Even with the same degree,
a white man is at least twice more likely
to be hired than you are.
So, can you really get far?
Are you actually allowed to bring quality to the table,
when you are repeatedly disabled
and purposely disenfranchised?
Can a Black man succeed, if he's always
despised
and colonised

by the powers that be?
People think, "Racism no longer exists here"
but it's just passive aggression, rooted in a fear,
that you'll figure out that you do matter.
They are scared you'll rise up and be your own master,
so, they label you violent and suspect,
hoping you'll keep quiet and respect their systems,
where they keep you on the bottom, chasing after crumbs.
Firing you, not hiring you, perpetually lying to you-,
mentally you can no longer progress.
Your brain needs a rest,
from the daily racism and micro-aggressions you face
from the self-constructed lie, also known as race.
Black man constantly struggling with economic exploitation.
Black man repeatedly told to ignore discrimination.
Black man subjected to too much prejudice and persecution.
Black man, your only way out it seems, is Revolution.

Rejected

He yearns to be accepted,
I guess, a common need
but somehow he was different,
look close, a troubled seed.
His wings were torn from battle,
his face a pool of scars,
his heart contained such pureness,
a soul they disregard.
His life has been a struggle,
he'll win but feels he's lost.
He'll manage to keep going,
despite life's winter frost.
His angels speak in numbers
to show they're always there.
Rejoice would be his glory
Instead, they wipe his tears.

Bully Boss

My new Manager is trying to
mess up my movements
but he is useless,
I wish he wouldn't do this!
I want to LOSE IT
but that would make excuses,
for them to get rid of me and leave me elusive,
bummed out at home,
searching on computers,
for another job.
I'm being mobbed, plus I'm muted!
Always been the type far from hype or abusive
but everywhere I go,
I meet this bunch of losers.
TOOTHLESS
with a bit of power,
now they're RUTHLESS.
Assume shit based on what they hear,
so they're mere STUDENTS.
And maybe I'm the teacher here,
"Fairness can't be tutored".
Or maybe it will end in tears, when someone
draws a Ruger?
But that's not my reality,
it can't be.
I just want a salary,
to take care of my family.
But why they always challenge me?
A black man
Raised in anarchy's finest academy
Jeez…

Great Heist

For centuries, the black man has
been humbled.
Stripped of his name, his dignity
and original language.
Taken from his home and displayed at auction,
whilst his Queen looks on,
knowing.

His wisdom, natural strength and endurance
consistently exploited for spiritual and financial
gain.
Having to work at least twice as hard
for recognition,
yet rarely being truly recognised.
The force he extends as an alpha,
contrasts to the submission that he ought
accept if he is to be 'successful'
in the place of work,
or when he comes home and turns the key.

The black man harbours pain like no other.
Silent screams can be heard
from his inner being,
as the culmination of continuous slights, irks
away at his soul.
Constantly frustrated,
fighting forces, losing a battle that
faith tells, "one day he will get the W".

The black man faces rejection when he sees his reflection.
His greatness heavily diluted by images of another black man's actions,
Tarnishing his.
This great deception...
Or myth,
is permeated through every media channel,
to perpetuate the great lie that everything black is bad.

When the narrative changes, the black man might get credit for his strength,
pace or sporting ability
but rarely for his intelligence, his ingenuity or his creativity.
It's a stitch-up from birth,
yet any mention of this curse,
is met with furious cries of, "he's pulling the race card again",
"He has a massive chip on his shoulder"
Or, "he is too soft, for not getting over his bloody past".
All in stark contrast to other atrocities,
where we are told we, "must never forget".
Black man, I see you.
I feel you.
I AM you.
Stay strong, my brother.

Kindness for Weakness

'The nicest fella you could meet',
Really I am,
But sometimes I get tested
For just being black, man.
Dark and I'm short
I figured God had a plan,
Cause some of the cards I was dealt,
It's like my life was a sham.
See, I've often been scammed
Someone's hand in my pocket,
I don't envy the rich
But if it was them, they would stop it,
Personal taxes we pay,
"Take my shirt
Leave me topless,"
A food bank ain't the answer
But piggy bank,
I see coppers.
I wasn't always this jobless.
I took pride in my efforts,
Always first
Guy at work,
Last to leave,
I was breathless.
But then
Meeting after meeting,
Undermined like a Jester,

See, I can deal with unkind
But why do I have to be peppered?
But no victim I am,
Rise strong like a weapon,
If it's a fight that they want,
"Roll up sleeves, let's do Tekken!"
I ain't taking no prisoners,
Cross me once
Keep it stepping,
But take kindness for weakness,
You'll think I grew up in Peckham!

Overcoming

Still I Rise

Up. Rise. Always
Like a bird in the treetop
Scoping
This life. My life
Broken
But still, I seek to rise

Rise, rise
Hoping
They loved
Show me devotion
Tears shed
I lacked emotion
But still, I will just rise

Rise, rise
Glory
They judged
They knew no story
Born black
And they deplored me
But still, I always rise.

False Reality

Feel like I'm living in a dream,
where reality isn't all it seems.
Where things I know should and would mean,
appear worthless like throwing money down a stream.
Similar to having access to truth,
that only you knew.
And the glue that held it together,
were impossibilities
and things you couldn't do.

Noosed by all the pressure,
like my ancestor, 'Sue'.
Wish I met her,
wonder was she promised some land?
Or perhaps a chance to do better?
Partner told he'd be bold, in control like Inspector?
Or did they both know their fate,
like my plate, sealed, to the letter?

A question to ask,
as I rise, to early start.
Know my boss doesn't feel me,
'cause I won't do his dance.
I can't do his dance.
Cold, two-step.
Chance be my last.

Chose to fly free like a bird
Caged.
Reality.
Contrast.

The Clever Monkey

Born in the year of the Monkey,
I grew up in this urban jungle city.
Had to learn how to navigate, can't hesitate,
can't take anyone's pity.
Had to learn who's willing to come on this
journey with me
and who would rather be alone,
take the pain and glory all on their own.
People make less sense, here in the animal
kingdom.
Mind games I always lost,
now I know how to win them.
Cotch, watch then branch out.
Interpret what I see.
They used to tell me "you're arrogant",
but that's only when they test me.
Have to work harder,
faster, smarter.
For some, see past my face,
I was born on the same street as you,
so why do I feel out of place?
The Zodiac year of the monkey,
that's what the calendar tells me:
Go through these struggles daily,
knowing.
I may never be free.

The Refugee

His life
Is like a journey
A path that never ends
His destiny is
Labelled
'The soul that never wins'
His heart remains divided
Each beat
Contains a sigh
Sometimes feels he's living -
Living just to die.
Don't know where he's going
This place
A foreign land
Boasted of its 'greatness'
He fails to understand
In life we all make choices
And reap what we have sown
If 'happy' is the measure
He feels it's time to go.

Wheel of Life

The only thing I've learned
is that I'll never stop learning
and if London's a prize wheel,
I promise it hasn't stopped turning.
I watch and I wait
Patience sought and not given,
a virtue but it helps me
in the fast-paced life that I'm living.

In this endless competition,
Spin the wheel,
for the thrill,
staying hopeful,
keeping vigilant,
it takes precision and skill.
What's it going to land on?
I wait and I
Wait.
Never what I planned on.
Twisted turnings of fate.

But no matter where the wheel lands,
I'll take that prize
and make it work,
Work smarter, sometimes harder.
I will get what I deserve.

Deep and Spiritual

Trials

The world is an illusion
A wise man taught me this
As people we lack courage
And live in life's abyss
The world is how you see it
We get what we give out
We dangle words like 'can't' and 'hard'
Yet wonder why we've naught
The world is an emotion glass
Half empty, filled with pain
We speak these phrases
Often
Then go through trials again
And again and again.

This World

This world is filled with energy
Ying, Yang
Came oh so close
In nature there are synergies
And beneath them lies our hope.

This world is filled with mystery
The surface is our illusion
The eyes don't guide the soul
This is the wrong conclusion.

The world is in division
To rule at any cost
We often miss the issue
They thrive when we are lost.

The world is filled with politics
The games that people play
They lure us with their freedoms
They take our rights away.

The world is how you see it
Perceive
Is our reality
A thin line can be grasped
Between genius and insanity

The World is filled with love
A feeling
words can't describe

It drifts in like the wind
And changes people's lives.

I Didn't Listen

They said that I was out there for myself
and that I didn't really care.
That I didn't really love 'em pure
and my motives were 'insincere'.
Accused me of having double standards,
and being a person they couldn't trust.
So, it's a good thing when I tell you,
I didn't listen much.

They said I should give up on my dreams,
the thoughts I hold so dear.
That life was just a 'struggle'
and fate could be so near.
They told me
"What you see is real, my friend,
Believe in what you touch".
So, it's a good thing when I tell you,
I didn't listen much.

They told me
Money was the source.
Working hard for 'P', "the only key",
That 'isms' didn't exist,
in a Meritocracy.
They told me accumulate this wealth,
in awe of Satan's love.
So, it's a good thing when I tell you,
I didn't listen much.

They told me

Religion was the way
and heaven was in the sky.
That God loved us all the same
and one day we would die.
They told me if we didn't live this way,
ablaze when we are judged.
So, it's a good thing when I tell you,
I didn't listen much.

The Lost Soul

They know that you exist
Your path was once so clear
The life that you exerted,
Was murdered through the years.
The sight is sore for many
That knew you as you were
The cause of so much envy
now distant like a blur.
Your fall from grace
Was sudden
Like a Star
Who lost his way.
"he makes the stage his own",
Is what they used to say.
A life of so much meaning
So vibrant
Like a sun.
Your confidence and
Warmth
Was clear, you were 'the one'.
The way you lived your life
No other could fill your shoes.
Taught me, "if you play, you win"
Whilst, "if you watch, you lose".
Race not for thy swift my friend
Endure at any cost.
Follow your inner voice
For without it, you are lost.

Inhuman

Lyrics are the way,
Artful expression contains the key,
Although we're not as human as we claim to be.
The devil lurks amongst us,
He hides in many guises,
His bitterness of self,
Prevents our souls from rising.
The poor are blessed with pain,
Disease and many questions.
We are judged
By our address,
much more than our confessions.
The truth is often hidden,
Whilst lies lay more exposed,
They move so indiscriminately
Between some friends and foes.
True love is what we seek,
Though pain is what we cling to.
Inclined to speak in words,
Though
Real power lies in symbols.

Star Seed

Up above
You gaze at us
At night, you seldom stay.
You guide us through
Our moments blue
When hardships reach our day.

You twinkle bright
No oversights
You never fail to shine
Your beauty deep
Beyond 'unique'
Exceeds all space and time.

They are calling out
In summer drought
For water and a star
They wish on you
Like prayers or food
Yet don't know who you are.

They call you names
And snap your face
Yet still you burst with pride
In truth, we should all model you
In how we live our lives.

A Poet's Journey

My Pen

Staring at a blank page
Poisoned pen
Poised to print
Paragraphs of pain
I aim
Target hit.
The page explodes on impact
Calm.

Poet

I am a Poet, don't you know it?
I speak with words that lift the hopeless,
I sing with birds that grace the ocean
And sometimes stoop to rouse emotion.
I am a wordsmith,
I'll have my time,
I couldn't last the daily grind.
I tried at first, the 9-5
But dreams lost pace,
Began to whine.

I am a Writer, this is my box
But sometimes get a 'Writer's block'
Where thoughts seize up in tangled knots
The head goes down,
My pen just stops.

A scriber's sphere,
No need to fear,
Will overcome
It might take years.
Commitments' made,
For pen to steer,
One thousand minds,
For one thousand years.

Keep Going

It's been forty days,
since he left his humble
beginnings.
He posts, "no J.O.B",
Losing heart fast,
plus, faith has deserted his path.
His feet reflect his restless journey,
They're bloody,
They're bruised,
They're sore.
His soles are weary,
Eyes are teary,
Yet still he yearns for more.
His Uni days seem far away,
as if they knew his fate,
A foreign land,
He overstands,
He should have known his place.
A lonesome journey, traipsed along,
"Will get the time of day",
He speaks those words aloud himself,
at night he kneels to pray.
His CV looks so dusty now,
amidst the summer sun,
His only want,
provide some grain,
plus rent,
He needs some crumbs,
Though quitters never win, was told.
Small mercy,

Saw off death,
He seems so close to giving in,
His life,
a scattered mess.
True artists live a troubled life,
'Tis strife can
be so cruel.
No resting now,
No furrowed brow,
"Keep going", is his rule.

On Reflection

Your debts are high
And life is dry,
You're poised to quit,
You can't get by.
You loved and lost,
You don't know why,
You sighed at first but now you cry.
Your money's low and days seem long,
You have no job and don't feel strong,
Your efforts fade and dreams are 'wrong'?
Yet wonder where your life has gone.

Alone

Alone up in my room I gaze,
Misplaced; an empty vessel,
The Mirror's glare reflects on me,
To think 'you were so special'.
A life of strife, where nothings nice,
Deep pain became engrained.
The bitter taste of lonely space,
Where only I can change.

My Advice

Explode them with your talents
Express your inner soul
Live life like it's golden
Be Captain
Take control.
Forget your troubled waters
And days that bear no fruit
Be true to all your values
And don't forget your roots
Keep true to special moments
Sweet thoughts, you must hold dear
Embrace a life of promise
Co-ordinate your fears
Beware those who wish you badness
And those that wish you hate
Be wise when pick your battles
And wise when choose your mates.

Relationships and Love

Imperfectly Perfect

Perfectly imperfect
Describes us much, so well
One moment, bliss, full, laughing
The next, we live in hell
We're beautifully broken
Two Bees who lost their wings
We rise, we glide in motion
Whilst caught in love's strong winds
Our struggles and our heartaches
Our pleasure, screaming pain
Our fighting and
Our healing,
Bestows our bond again.

Who Wins?

If someone always has to win,
you'll never find true balance within.
A society of people on top, wanting to hold that position
of privilege, success, superior power.
The people underneath want to take it from them.

A constant battle.
Value drops and then it rises,
we need to act like people, not stock market prices.
What determines your worth? Gender, race, your income?
These superficial successes not difficult to see through;
inside is a good man who seriously needs you.

Feminism strengthens some,
used wrong, crushes others.
Soaring rates of mental illness consume sons, fathers, brothers;
men in their own right, not their worth to another.

Suicide rates climb higher, no mercy; a path of self-destruction.
Drugs and alcohol, addictions,
used just to function.

Anti-depressants, divorce rates,
no love to give or received.
In this independent society we pretend;
we only see our own needs.

Children raised never seeing affection in their homes.
From birth they journeyed through life's
ills on their own.

Thrown into a dangerous society.
filled with violence and cruelty
by parents that used to be in love
but now times are harder,
hardly speak.

Whilst some freeze out their partner,
Quick as they scarper
for a thrilling encounter,
So tempted to cheat

From Millens to Gen Z,
Pray they stand a chance,
When God's presence is muted,
We watched devils dance.

Pretending
things are ok – they're not
but they could be.
As brothers and sisters,
RISE!
Let's rise and make history.

Set the Rabbit Free

A rabbit in the den of the lion,
watched by a predator's narrow eyes.
Harsh life as a prey animal, always on the run.
Who do you trust? Who do you flee from?
Is he a tinder date, or a future murderer?
She trusted someone who just wanted to hurt her.
Abusive relationships, over time, people change,
from a caring lover to a tyrant, full of rage.
Recognise the signs, know when to leave;
you have to be assertive to get what you need.
Set yourself free,
don't pretend they will change.
That's no reason to stay.
Women discover a talent for makeshift weapons,
cute handbag tasers, key-chain rape whistles.
The useless excuse of, "he won't do it again."
Repeated over and over again.
You might not be at fault but understand,
that the power to stop this is in your hands.
All that it takes is just one bad man,
to destroy a woman's dignity
or end her life;
threaten her with a gun or a knife.
There are hundreds of men like these.
Men like these,
BOYS like these!
Bringing society down to its knees.

It takes only one good man to stop him.
Prove you are one of them.
Be the good Lion.
Set the Rabbit free.

Travel

The Traveller

Violence became so dogmatic
being raised in the Southside of London
Like being caught in a rip-current and there is
no illusion
Trapped inside a world of darkness you ask, "Is
this all there is to Life?"
The thought-provoking question that leaves the
heart and mind in strife
Stepping away from the streets, as hope begins
to lose its shape
Searching for an escape, you feel your soul
begin to wake
Every step a new experience, a journey etched
in memory
A spark lights up the darkness, to reveal life's
hidden treasury
Open Heart, Open Mind, Open Eyes, now I
finally see
Beauty indescribable and adventures that set
you free
Through the path of the Traveller,
I found the beauty within me.

Black Man in Thailand

Stepping off the plane and landing in Bangkok,
The name alone was a giveaway to some of the fun that was in store.
I entered my hotel and the warm greeting from the starry-eyed receptionist,
Made me know that it could be on.
Plus, she was so pretty and fine.
I dropped my cases off and headed out to hit the
Bustling Bangkok streets,
Skipping along in my mind, as if I was a child again.
'Chocolate Man'
'Chocolate Man'
I see a sea of beautiful Thai women,
Uttering words, I'd usually take offence to but not in Thailand.
Never in Thailand.
It's as if the warmness of the words, made the chocolate melt.
Not fully but to the point that I am now
In a juxtaposed position.
I love her and I hate her at the same.
But then one of the girls sees the confusion on my face
And utters those famous Thai Words,
Healing, comforting words that end division
And diversity
Amongst humans,
"Same, same but different".

'What does that mean?', I thought, as one of the girls
Brushed her skinny little arm against mine,
Contrasting our complexions
As one, intertwined.
Thailand taught me how to be free.
How to get up every day and smile,
Despite what life throws at you.
How to make a little go a long way.
How to hustle harder and keep the faith,
Even when the universe conspires against you.
Thailand.
I love you.

Scraping the Sky

Utopia learned how to build on top of itself,
growing higher and higher.
Friday brunches, mimosas, and you'll always get
pleasantly drunk by lunch.
Utopia learned how to forget
and the city is happy to teach you; it's very easy
to learn its tricks.
If you build with resources that aren't yours,
You'll excel your path to rich.
Swimming with thousands who are just like you,
same dreams, same city.
In the water's artificial blue, perfectly polluted
with hopeful tourists,
Those wanting to change their lives forever,
they just get lost.
Continuous border runs; Visa's 60 days expire,
that's
the price paid for the dream.
Don't want to wake up from it, or maybe you
forgot how to wake up?
Born a different colour, different race and
Utopia
forgets sympathy... empathy.
Working too many hours but for no job security.
It's a dream you chased;
a dream you paid for with money and
everything
else you own, too.
Party on the beaches, constructed soullessly for
your enjoyment.

The waves take your love, your time, your sorrow,
out to a sea of plastic.
Utopia knows how to take your passion, your energy
and sends you home empty.
You paid thousands for a dream but got a nightmare
you can't exchange.
No refund, no receipt and the store is closed now.
The sky is falling now.
Utopia learned how to build on top of its workers, their lives;
they sink under its weight.
Utopia grows higher and higher and higher on top of them;
it pushes them down,
after promising to bring them to the top of its skyscrapers.
They'll never touch the sky.

Ethiopian Goddess

It started with you, Ethiopia
The motherland
Forgotten place
Where sacred souls
Harmoniously exist
Drinking roasted coffee out of rusty coffee cups
And donning the biggest smiles

Ethiopia, you are the only place in Africa that
they couldn't colonise
Couldn't break down or
Dilute, as your culture seeps through
Every taste of the Amharic tongue
Off the lips into the churches and dance steps
you wear so well

I dreamt of you Ethiopia
Reuniting with my past
Sharing stories with acquaintances
Now ancient friends
As if they knew my soul

My ancestors will be proud that I made this
journey, Ethiopia
amongst the contrasting
Fleet of brown colour complexions
the mind can muster

Into the heart of your beating city
Laid bare for all to embrace.

Ethiopian Goddess,
Your pride and soul will never be erased.

Freedom

Jamaican Sunrise

Blinded by tribulations, caught up in self-reprise
Lost in bitter darkness, staring at treacherous skies
Birthing inner demons, with no will exorcise
I was saved by the warming light of a Jamaican Sunrise
With an effervescent beauty that captivates the mind
Birthing energy to resurrect a fallen heart
Warming atoms into existence
The symbol of a brand-new fresh start.
When lost in the fear of night
The pink sky empowers us to rise when we fall
And like a smile, it is contagious
A Sunrise exists within us all.

A New Age

A new age
Is upon us,
Embrace it, don't be scared.
For the life we once encompassed,
Will be lost like no one cared.
The truth
Was once so sacred,
Appears before our eyes.
Two thousand years of darkness,
Illuminated by glistening lights.
Communities reap
Pure harvests,
Good deeds
Were not forgotten.
No longer will we languish in lands,
Resembling Gotham.
The devil we know so well,
He lurks in many guises,
Will finally be defeated
As humanity exorcises.
A lie was told, too many,
Blind faith, a source 'unknown',
Let us
Rejoice this travesty,
As forever
Is being shown.

Finally Free

I am finally free,
the chains that anchored
My soul are no more.
My Ancestors look on from distant lands
Applauding the rise of this brave bold soldier.
I'm free.
Free to rise amongst the challenges that I face,
Free to pace up and down
Waving my banner of change and not care who is watching.
I'm free.
Free like a Daffodil
Roaming roughshod over a cotton field,
Where my ancestors grinded,
Working the land,
Whilst concocting their plans of escape.
I'm free, free like the power to tell you to, "P Off", if you test me,
Knowing that Massa isn't here to beat down my spirit,
Or punish me for not obeying his every command.
I'm free, like the air we breathe on a breezy day or
Dancing on the stage of life,
Whilst young children play out in the rain.
I am free, like the word pain doesn't exist,
And free love flourishes freely amongst my fellow friends
I am Free!

I am Free!
I am finally Free!

Family Ties

Mother's Day

The weight on this woman's shoulders,
The tears that she has cried,
The nurturing and love she shares,
Much more than words recite.

The tasks that she accomplishes,
The praise that goes untold,
The grace that she embraces,
As if she's made of gold.

A gift that she was blessed with,
A curse she feels sometimes,
But rarely does she grumble,
Instead, she simply shines.

A mother's heart expands,
Through everything she does,
I know we've fought like Lions,
But Ma, you are my Love!

Grandma

I sometimes think of you; our bond, the time we shared.
The way you used to hold me close,
When I thought that no one cared.
Your presence in our family,
A Matriarchal,
Who, 'knew the way',
You gave me strength and courage,
When disappointments
Came my way.
Shorter than you were,
No soul could claim as 'fierce'
But look what you achieved,
The love that you have reared.
Your children miss you dearly,
Your grandkids do the same,
You see it in our eyes,
We've grown, matured with age.
A disciple of discipline,
My Mum became your clone,
She's "real" like you as well
And sweet like a Shakespeare poem.
I'll never forget you Gran
And know I'll see you soon,
Save me a place in heaven,
Besides the brightened moon.

Old Skool Rhymes
(Back in the day)

Blame Satan

I came in this game
Like flames in the rain,
They tried to douse me out
But my pain was a stain.
You talk to any hustler,
The names might have changed
But the thing that stays the same,
Is the rage in the brain.
"I gotta hustle harder,
Get the fame," then I fade.
Has never been my story
I'm amazing with blades.
Meaning that I'm sharper,
Got the A's when I trained,
Now I get the P's in,
An AP is in Range,
Now they wanna play me,
Like my name was Hussein
But who's sane in this world,
Where young babies are slain?
Papers are faked
Every day for the 'flakes',
Now the state of the peeps
Is sheep behind a gate,
Wait.
Look a likkle deeper,
And it's bait
And it won't be long before
You're turning on your mates,
In a place

Where the Skunk gets laced,
Like it's Mace.
Yet another funeral 'cause
He made this mistake.
Baby mum crying
Tried to shame a bro to change.
Now he's in his cell, denying
But "his ways were his ways,"
Perhaps he didn't see it,
Like a snake that's inane,
But
Now he's serving life
And, "Satan's to blame".

No Love

It's hard to find the love,
on the streets, oh Lord.
See them hustling
on the corners,
ain't no eats for the poor.
When you go up in that fridge
and that feeling is your
tummy rumble,
'cause you can't afford to go store.
And this money trouble
makes you wanna hustle, juggle,
crying to your peeps, 'cause you didn't
wanna struggle struggle.
Finding you're a Leech,
when all you saw was little cuddles.
Dying to defeat
but you're down on your knees,
now you cry in your sleep,
'cause the mind is so deep.
Fortified by the guys,
with their eye on your lease.
Go survive in the beast,
when the 9s done increased,
4-5 rise, hide or lie in a heap,
breathe a sigh of relief,
'cause the 9th of the week.
Go sign, fine, now you're buying a quiche,
is the life of a Neek
but I've been here many times.
Economy sucks

like Brexit down the line
but it's fine.

R.I.P Souljah

He hurts from the inside,
life took away his pride.
somewhere down the line, we watched as he lost his stride.
Used to be living nice plush places, him and guys,
tough, they were living life.
Running round and catching vibes,
chillin' with the older guys,
raving like, every night.
Other guys would try it, so they ended up in plenty fights.
People used to buy shit and tell them it would get them high.
The next thing you know, they're spending money that should get them by.
His boy was much worse though, blazing from day to night,
I really should've gauged it, from the way he used to slant his eyes.
He was an actor,
Disguised things, like little mice.
Or is that the guilt,
for not being there when he skyed,
April 10th, got a call that would change one's life:
"M, X has passed"
said a voice on the other line,
"He's just OD'd, police on scene, it was Heroin".
I really don't believe this,

"My God!"
His soul will never die!

Ancestors' Blood

Always walk head high,
Heart on my sleeve.
Ancestors' blood and the soul of a G,
Yet sometimes I find myself praying in these streets.
Like, what's wrong with peeps?
They're shooting in Mackey D's!
Far from the good,
We need a remedy.
Charged with a Zute and drinking Hennessy,
Do "they" laugh
When they see this truthful imagery?
Always got time for mo' conspiracies.
Barbers be telling me gossip up in my seat
But we don't snitch,
So, nothing will be repeat.
We don't think this weather
Will ever cease
So, we just party.
I'm loving Miss Sudanese,
Chances
I'll get her loving me 'tween the sheets,
Dancing
'neath stars,
Is this called 'heavenly'?
Laughing, 'cause this could be
So devilishly,
Perceived when we up
in the back of my Cherokee.

Fed Up

We all need daily bread,
And by that, I mean dough
But downsizing is in fashion,
The 'in' for a business to grow.
Lose, win,
What is the difference
As long as businesses flow?
Automation,
AI, inflation,
Soon, we'll be losing our homes.
And the leaders will they feed us,
When they're preaching us 'hope'?
I saw the smirk behind your smile
And know your reaching for votes.
I know the answer is 'nope'!
"Get in, make those pound notes,"
Then make us worship celebs,
"I bet they won't even know".
See I've seen past this charade,
Like my mind was a scope,
Third eye is always open,
Always preeing these folks.
A per cent could make the difference,
Between shelter and clothes
And end the word, 'starvation'
Like it didn't evolve.
But it didn't evolve.
See us living in woes,
Remnants of broken systems
where we do what we're told,

Wasn't slavery the same?
I guess we minus the boats.
Throw on a little shirt
And now we're sticking our nose
Up, at other people
Like, "check so and so",
"What he do again?"
"I saw him sweeping the road" (Whisper)
"What you do again?"
Uttered some ting on a pole, imagine.
"Babe, mind your business,
That's the key to your goals!"

The Eye of the Hurricane

I'm like the Eye of the Hurricane,
I may seem sane
But around me,
Shit's rowdy.
Checked the weather report,
'More than a bit cloudy'.
Plus, I've got all these heads,
That chat about me.
Will I reign?
Or will I get slain,
In an Audi?
TT preferably.
Some want to see the death of me,
And I ain't even making Ps,
Peeps want me to R.I.P,
From G's to corrupt Police,
But I will never 'freeze'.
So, tell me with these cards
Laid out,
What the outcome will be?
Black Man.

About the Author

Maximus is a writer, motivator and free thinker. He was born in 1980 and grew up in Thornton Heath, Croydon. He has travelled extensively and spent a number of years living and working in the Middle East. He graduated from the University of the West of England and obtained a Business Administration degree. He is 40 years old and resides in Bristol, UK.

Epilogue

I wrote this book to help people in all walks of life, at a time where natural disasters are on the increase, wars are ever-present and suicide rates and mental health issues amongst men, are at an all-time high, not to mention Covid-19, which is changing society as we know it.

With the additional rise of automation and AI technology, there are likely to be substantial job losses, increasing the pressure in the home, so as people we need encouragement and motivation more than ever before.

My aim is to highlight some of our realities through words, then attempt to uplift people through channelled wisdom, experience and foresight, encouraging strength, will and bold action in the epic but uncertain future that awaits us all.

Reflection Notes

www.ingramcontent.com/pod-product-compliance
Lightning Source LLC
Chambersburg PA
CBHW020447220526
45464CB00002B/896